Thomas, this is dedicated to you.

Luke, Christina, Johnny, Katie, Robert, Patty, and Tony, this is because of you.

Anthony and Riley, I am of you.

I am of You by Carolyn Richards
Copyright © 2025 Carolyn Richards

All rights reserved. No part of this book may be reproduced in any form or by an electronic or mechanical means without permission in writing from the publisher, except by a reviewer who may quote a brief passage in a review.

This is a work of fiction. Names, characters, places, and incidents are the product of the author's imagination. Any resemblance to actual persons, events, or locales, is entirely coincidental.

ISBN 979-8-9917538-3-8 (Paperback)
ISBN 979-8-9917538-4-5 (Hardcover)
ISBN 979-8-9917538-5-2 (eBook)

Library of Congress Control Number 2024924621

Cover Design by Moran Reudor
Illustrated by Moran Reudor
Published by RyAnt Studio

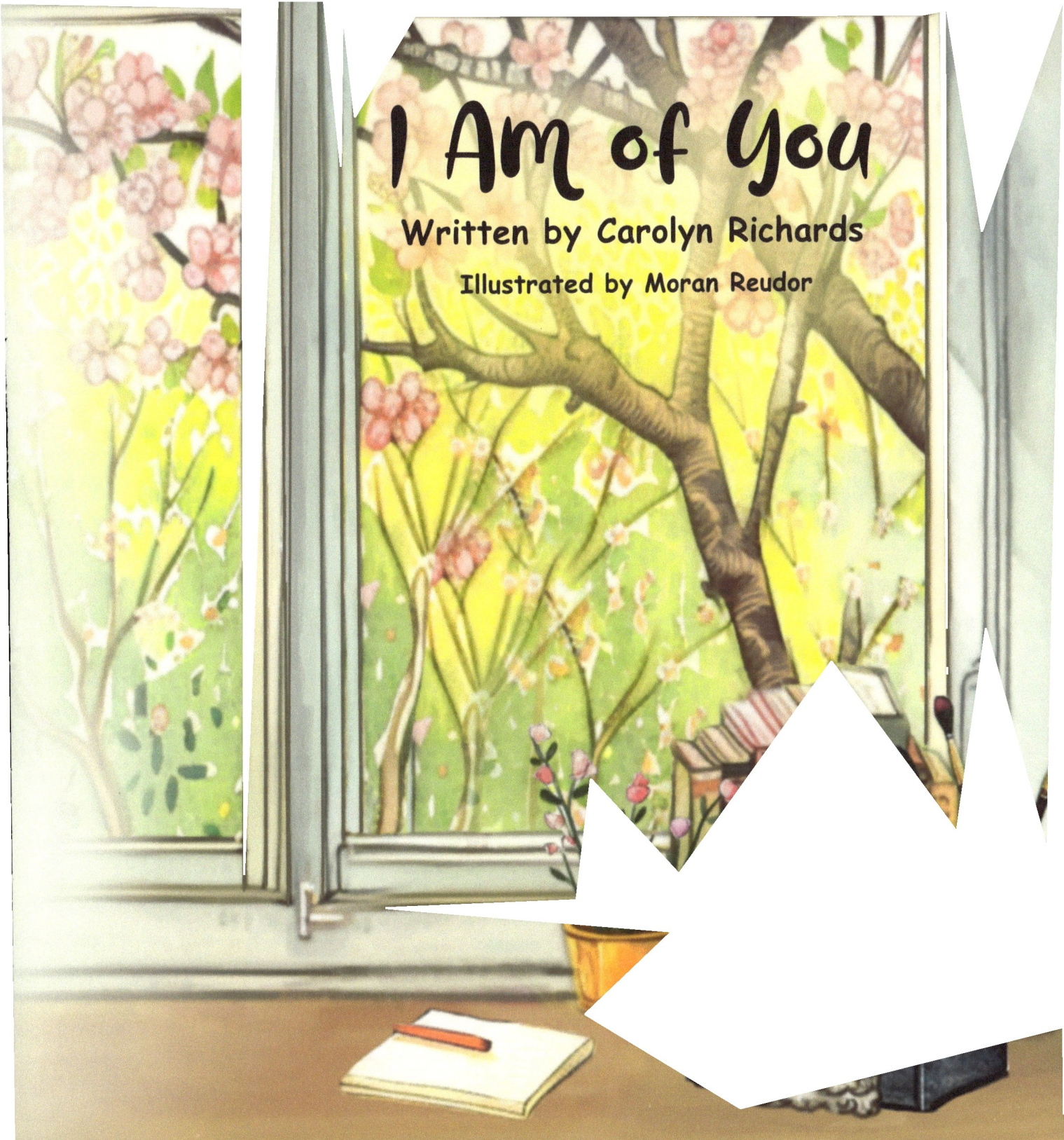

You wrote a letter to me one gentle evening
in May. You wrote me letters for my birthday
every year, but this one seemed to
be written for no particular reason.
And, it is my favorite.

You used a notepad sized
paper and wrote on
one page front and back.
It had been a few years
since I last read it,
but I knew where to find it.

I always knew where to find it.

I took the weathered letter
from my small tin of keepsakes
and began to read.
I turned the letter over
and at the top of the page
you wrote, "I am of you."

I paused. Although you
wrote that *you are of me*,
I began to think how *I am of you*.

I am of the confidence you instilled each time I took the field.

I am of the encouragement you gave when I thought I was not enough.

I am of the family vacations you planned that rarely went as planned.

I am of the spark you gave people
who were feeling down
and needed those "just right" words.

I am of the patience you showed
when my heart broke
for the first time.

I am of the intensity you
emanated when you reminded
me of my worth.

I am of the creativity you shared through your jokes and stories.

I am of your epic air drum solos.
I am of the laughter you gifted a room.

I am of the quiet you provided
when I needed to think.

I am of the conviction you conveyed
during difficult conversations.

I am of the resilience you demonstrated
when people tried to get you down.
And they sometimes did.

I am of the times you let me win,
and even more so of the times you did not.

I am the culmination of
your highs,
   your lows,
      your presence,
         and absence.

With a small smile and warmed heart,
I gently placed the letter back in the tin.

May came
around again.

I found the small tin,
and as I did many times before,
began to read the weathered letter.
But this time was different.

I noticed something. I felt something.
My fingers ran across a crease at the
top of the page.

I am of yo

You must know how absolutely proud I am of you

I slowly unfolded the crease to find your intended message to me all those years ago.

You wrote, "You must know how absolutely proud I am of you."

Proud.
You were proud of me.

And Dad,

I am of you.

www.ingramcontent.com/pod-product-compliance
Lightning Source LLC
Chambersburg PA
CBHW041135130526
44582CB00031B/125